Ana,
Thank you for supporting my work.
~KB

terms & conditions

THE FINE PRINT TO AN ANTI-RACIST SOCIETY

Dr. Kiara Butler

WHITESIDE PUBLISHING

Whiteside Publishing is an independent publishing company that specializes in the production of Christian and self-help books.

Las Vegas, Nevada

terms & conditions by Kiara Butler
Senior Editor: Briana Whiteside
Published by Whiteside Publishing
Las Vegas, Nevada
For inquiries, please visit:
www.brianawhiteside.com

Graphic Designer: EMBB Designs

terms & conditions

DISCLOSURES

I write this book from the heart, soul, and wounds of a queer, same-gender-loving, Black woman navigating the complexities of our society. I write through the experiences that remind me of what I am up against: a world that discriminates against the LGBTQ community, Black people, and women, each social construct in which my identity intersects.

As a collective, I hope you sit with the feelings and emotions that may come up as you navigate this book, taking time and space as needed. But most importantly, I hope you take this book as truth.

Black women, I hope as you navigate this book, you feel seen, heard, and supported to live fully in your skin.

The Black community, I hope as you navigate this book, you can create a space beyond these pages for your Blackness too.

Black families, I hope as you navigate this book, you find the courage to have conversations that have been generationally rooted in fear.

Survivors of abuse, I hope as you navigate this book, you find peace in the truth that it wasn't your fault.

Queer folx, I hope as you navigate this book, you are able to let go of the internalized messages from society that may cause you to not show up in your fullness.

White folx, I hope as you navigate this book, you acknowledge that the work of creating an anti-racist society is yours to do. And in that acknowledgment, you identify your contributions to all the ways in which we, as a society, exist.

To my unborn child, I did this work for you.
This book is for you.

I love you already and I can't wait to meet you.

CONTENTS

CONTRIBUTION CLAUSE

This book has been in the works for a couple of years now. I've written it in my mind more than a thousand times, and I'm happy I finally get to share it with the world.

Thank you, Dr. Briana Whiteside, for standing in your passion and creating a company that pushes writers, specifically Black writers, to use their voices in spaces where we have been historically silenced. I am so grateful to have worked with Whiteside Publishing and could not have crafted this book without your expertise and guidance.

To my early reviewers, Dr. Celeste Bowler, Molly Cohen, and Dr. David Johns thank you for taking time out of your busy schedules to read and make recommendations. Believe it or not, reading your responses really helped motivate me to get this book across the finish line.

Thank you, Precious Lopez, for responding to my reflection exercises even though the content was heavy and required us to do so over drinks. I'm not even sure how Jael Lopes dealt with my line of questioning daily.

Ya'll both helped to ensure I wrote the workbook with intention.

Lastly, to the people behind the scenes: Advancing Agency, Cat Laine, Diversity Talks, EMBB Designs, and Powers Solutions, I can't thank ya'll enough for putting up with my shenanigans during the writing process.

We did it, ya'll! This is for us.

INTRODUCTION

ACCPEPTABLE CLAUSE

Reader,

I want to take you on a journey with me, but before I take you on this journey, I have to trust you with my life.

The rules are simple.
They are pretty straightforward, actually.
Even still, I should mention that this work won't be easy; anti-racism work never is.

On this journey, I have the responsibility of:

1. modeling vulnerability

    1.1   To ground us in this work, I will model vulnerability by incorporating my personal experiences within each chapter. Some portions of this book were challenging for me to process and write, but those very emotions are what assured me that I was doing the internal work needed to create an anti-racist society.

2. calling a thing a thing

2.1 *Developing a common language is essential in discussing racism and other forms of oppression in the United States. Therefore, I will call a thing and thing by providing terms and definitions for each chapter. Make note that the descriptions of some terms may be different from your day-to-day usage.*

3. taking accountability for my actions

3.1 *Creating an anti-racist society requires us to identify how we individually contribute to inequitable systems. Throughout this book, I will dissect the layers of my identity and lived experiences and name where I have intentionally or unintentionally contributed to white supremacy.*

4. providing you with resources and tools

4.1   *We can easily overlook the work required to create an anti-racist society. Therefore, within this book and the accompanying workbook, I will provide critical takeaways hidden within the fine print, frequently asked questions as knowledge assessments, and reflection exercises as resources on your anti-racist journey.*

On this journey, you have the responsibility of:

1. navigating the chapters in order

1.1   *There is no finish line for gaining cultural competence, and it is not a linear journey. I designed this book and the accompanying workbook, to be read and completed in chronological order. Therefore, I encourage you to refrain from skipping ahead without doing the work required in the previous chapters. Remember, once you've completed a chapter, you can always revisit what you've read.*

2. using the accompanying workbook

2.1   *The accompanying workbook is your compass, so don't rush the process and take as much time as you need with the reflection exercises. It is also important to familiarize yourself with the Terms & Conditions within each chapter before moving on to the next chapter.*

3. leaning into discomfort

3.1   *Real change only happens when you reach a level of discomfort, and only you know when you've gotten to that level. So challenge yourself to be vulnerable as you read, learn, unlearn, and reflect. Remember, part of doing the work is sitting in the discomfort, so I encourage you to hold the tension.*

4. holding yourself accountable

4.1   *It's easy to place blame on outside factors without doing the internal work of acknowledging your contribution, so when considering the ways in which you've accepted the Terms & Conditions of our society, try to refrain from excusing your behaviors during this process. We all must accept responsibility if we hope to change.*

I think that is it.

And it's okay...
You don't have to be nervous.
You don't have to feel like you have to have it
all figured it out.

I've taken this journey before and by taking
you with me, I hope we can collectively work
together to create an anti-racist society.

But before we go, I do think it's important to
mention here that the Terms & Conditions of
our society will benefit who they are supposed
to and, well, you'll learn more about the Terms
& Conditions **when** and **only** if you agree to
come where I am about to take you.

So, do you agree to come?

Terms and Conditions ('Terms')

As promised, here are some key terms to get you started. As you continue to navigate through the book and respond to the reflection exercises in the workbook, try to incorporate the terms into your responses and day-to-day interactions. By developing a common language, we will be able to engage in dialogue with others with the assurance that confrontation or conflict is not a result of misinterpretation.

Anti-Racist: continuously self-reflecting on individual contributions to injustice on a micro, meso, and macro-level by unlearning and learning how racism operates within the United States and actively addressing and condemning it when witnessed.

Institutional Power: the societal approval given to a governing entity to control and make decisions on behalf of other people.

Non-Racist: acknowledging that racism exists within the United States, while still holding individual power by separating self from racism and not condemning it when witnessed.

Prejudice: a preconceived, unfair, and unreasonable opinion, usually formed without knowledge, that often leads to violent or hateful behaviors.

Racism: any prejudice held or discrimination committed against a racial group that is reinforced by systems of power.

Systems of Oppression: discriminatory institutions, structures, and norms that are embedded within and reinforced by the structures of our society.

Rules of Conduct

I pulled up to the Department of Human Services in Rhode Island around 8:00 am. I had thirty minutes to spare until they were scheduled to open because one of my girlfriends informed me that the lines were always long, so I wanted to arrive early. Even with the online application that I submitted, there were still steps that I had to complete in person. After going through the metal detectors and following the hallway signs and arrows, I finally made it to *the rumored line*. Nervously waiting with all of my documents sorted and labeled in folders, I zoned in and out of consciousness as the line inched forward. Just as I was starting to calculate how much longer my legs would keep me standing, a voice from the back office called what sounded like my name.

"Key-are-uh"
"Key-air-ah"
"Key-are-ah"

The caseworker repeated herself in a failed attempt to place the correct syllable emphasis. It was a Black woman. She couldn't have been over fifty years old and wore nice tight curls that hadn't fallen yet; she was looking real jazzy for a Monday morning. Though it was only 10:00 am, I could tell she was already over being at work that day. She didn't say much to me as we migrated away from the line. She just walked me back to her desk and handed me a stack of papers to sign.

"It honestly doesn't matter what it says. Shit. I've been in line for two hours," I told myself.

While sitting at her desk, signing page after page of the never-ending documents, I noticed that she made eye contact with me for the first time in the 15 minutes that I had been sitting there.

"You don't belong here. You will find a job in no time," she said.

"Finally... Somebody recognizes my worth," I thought to myself.

I smiled and told her, *"Thank you."*

Honestly, I wasn't really sure how to respond to her affirmation statement. I had just stood for hours in line, and now I was sitting at her desk being interviewed to receive government assistance. Internally, I felt like a failure and was embarrassed for having to rely on government assistance, but there was something about her telling me that I didn't belong in that place that made me question *who belongs there* and who gets to decide?

"Where do you currently live?
Elderly/Disabled Housing?
Homeless: lobby, street, car?
Shelter/Halfway House?
Living in another's home/apartment?
Drug/Alcohol rehab center?," she asked.

It took me a while to even tell her that I was living with a friend because I was trying to make sense of who was responsible for creating this list of housing options. I started to wonder if my nerves were just getting to me, causing me to be skeptical of every little detail. I tried to silence the voices telling me to believe otherwise, but as she made her way through my application, I couldn't help but feel "shitty." That was the only word to categorize how I felt completing a government assistance application that didn't even provide an option for what would be considered *stable housing.*

"Is any applicant imprisoned? If so, at what facility and when will they be released?" she followed.

Questions similar to these continued to be riddled throughout the rest of the application, and the subtleness of collecting my demographic information that could negatively categorize my Blackness was alarming. Interestingly, the manipulative framing of the caseworker's questions intentionally positioned me experiencing food insecurity, homelessness, or imprisonment as a norm of Blackness. Once the caseworker finished confirming that the answers I provided on my application matched my verbal responses, it was time for me to sign the rules of conduct in order to receive my benefits. To be clear, I didn't feel as if I was benefiting at all, though. In fact, the entire process made me feel less than and as if this route was my only option. The government designed the system to make those in need feel this way; it is not accidental. For people who have never endured the lengthy process, consider the application that is not representative of who you are, the line that I believe is intentionally longer than the DVM lines, and the interrogation that individuals endure as if everyone is attempting to milk the system. There's an irony in how we view and talk about government assistance as a society.

I must admit that I vaguely remember what any of the latter portion of the application asked beyond the legal jargon:

"You have the right to..."

"You have the responsibility to..."

I was focused on making it through the interrogation. I told myself I had made it through, and the hard part was over. However, as I was leaving the building with my emergency stamps totaling $250.00 in hand, I remembered to take a closer look at the people waiting for caseworkers to interview them. Essentially, I wanted to see if I could differentiate between *who belonged and who didn't*. That was a difficult task.

Here's what I remember: Women of color and some with children peopled the line that extended at least three blocks down the hall. I couldn't really tell their circumstances from looking at them, but the Department of Human Services had already labeled everyone in the line part of the system. I felt their labeling in the application questions. I saw it in the way the staff looked at us. I heard it in their condescending tones when people asked simple questions like the location of the restroom. And yet, the only responsibility we had in confirming and accepting that label was to check the box, sign a stack of papers, and appreciate whatever was given to us by the system's workers.

Do you ever take the time to read the Terms & Conditions?

Did you accept the Terms & Conditions of our society?

Later that day, I prepared to go to the grocery store for the first time using food stamps. I had already gotten the most challenging part out of the way, I kept telling myself, so this part should be easy. I went down my usual aisles at the store, grabbed my everyday staple foods, and made my way to the nearest checkout. Finally, I secured my items.

The lines of the open registers were long, and every self-checkout register that seemed to be moving slightly faster had handwritten signs plastered with *"Sorry, no EBT'"* on them. When I shopped with cash in the past, I never paid much attention to the signs. I was always able to navigate the store freely without restrictions and a sign blatantly telling me that I didn't belong, or that I was no longer afforded convenience because I was using EBT. After doing a couple of laps back and forth between aisles, surveying how many groceries people had in their carts, plus how quickly the cashier was able to scan and bag, I finally chose to stand in line with maybe three people ahead of me.

Time seemed to go by fairly quickly as I waited. I may have been comparing my time in the grocery line to the two hours I waited in line at the Department of Human Services. It is also possible that the line seemed to quickly move because I spent the time contemplating whether or not I deserved M&Ms. Yet, before I knew it, I was putting my groceries on the conveyor belt and making my way towards my bags. I handed the cashier my membership card, and I watched as the grocery total climbed and fell as discounts were applied.

"Your total is $116.29," the cashier said.

As I was reaching into my wallet to grab the EBT card that I ensured was active and ready to use ten minutes before leaving home, I was working hard to accept my current reality as truth. But, it wasn't until it was time for me to actually use the card that the familiar feelings of embarrassment and shame that I was previously clinging to just hours earlier came rushing back to me like a boomerang.
As a result, I quickly swiped the card while trying to position my fingers over any evidence that it was EBT. While I'm not even entirely sure who was around to witness this act, at that moment, for some reason, it felt like every single person in the store was watching me. Pointing at me. Judging me. I immediately felt like an imposter. There's a complex nuance in how I was feeling. A part of me was ashamed that I was someone who needed government

assistance, while a part of me felt like I was above *those people* who needed it to survive.

Maybe that's what the caseworker meant. I didn't fit the profile of a person who needed food stamps. *At least, not in the ways that we're taught. As I pulled out of the parking lot into the evening traffic, I told myself that, "...maybe my feelings of embarrassment were just confirming that truth."*

When I made it home to put the groceries away, it was around 5:00 pm, which was just long enough for the day's embarrassment to subside. Thankfully, it was also long enough for me to attempt to strategize my way out of food insecurity and into the high-paying job society had promised me my entire life.

I wasn't lazy and uneducated.

I wasn't just trying to live off of the system like society says.

Mental ruminations.

That is the subtleness of living in a racist society.

Even if the Terms & Conditions negatively impact you directly or indirectly, enough people in our country have already agreed to them. They have accepted the privileges they provide while the *rest of us* are the liability.

To live in an anti-racist society means to be willing to speak up against policies and laws that harm other people, even if you aren't the one directly impacted. It is to unlearn information and processes that continue to replicate systems of oppression. It is also taking accountability for your contributions to these systems, whether intentionally or unintentionally.

We are all responsible.

I wrote *Terms & Conditions: The Fine Print to an Anti-Racist Society* for all of these reasons. I want us to have the ability to identify and assume responsibility for our contributions to injustice. Additionally, I want us to be able to collectively do this work, as communities, as families, and as individuals.

The journey of outwardly creating an anti-racist society is first and foremost an internal one.

Governing Law

Each chapter of this book is governed by one of the four dimensions of the PERM Framework: Power, Empathy, Relationships, and Mindset. The PERM Framework is a-first-of-its-kind methodology that builds on the established Cultural Competence Continuum, which is widely used in education as a teacher coaching tool (Lindsey et al., 2009). In 2019, I expanded this coaching tool as a part of my Doctorate in Education research to provide a roadmap for reflection on cultural norms, biases, behaviors, and how these factors impact other people. In each chapter, we will do this work together using a protocol known as "**I do, we do, you do**."

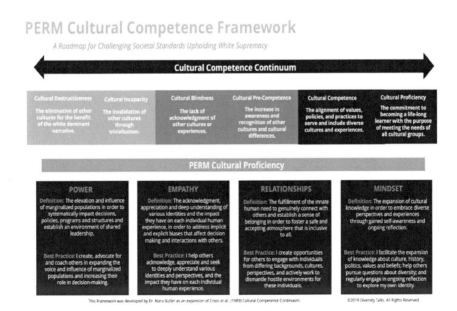

Each chapter will begin with an open letter related to one of the four PERM dimensions **(I do),** followed by context as to how our acceptance of the terms and conditions of our society has a lasting impact **(we do)**. At the end of each chapter, you will then use the accompanying workbook to answer a series of reflection exercises based on the critical takeaways and content of the chapter **(you do)**.

Chapter 1
Power: What Are You Willing to Lose?

Through the lens of power, we will navigate through the process of understanding our acceptance of the social hierarchy. We will explore a real-life experience where power and control tactics are used before dissecting how power dynamics exist within our society.

Chapter 2
Empathy: Can Multiple Narratives Exist?

Chapter two is designed to help us navigate the process of understanding the social impact of racial stereotypes on our ability to express authentic empathy. We will explore a real-life experience from a unique perspective before dissecting our acceptance of the societal pressures for resilience.

Chapter 3
Relationships: Are You Really Well?

In this chapter, we will navigate through the process of identifying societal messages and norms that may influence our ability to form genuine relationships. We will explore a real-life experience highlighting the importance of having our innate needs met before dissecting how this translates into our interactions in society.

Chapter 4
Mindset: At Whose Expense?

During this chapter, we will navigate through the process of identifying how societal messages and norms influence our behavior and mindset. We will explore a real-life experience from the perspective of self before dissecting the internalization of societal messaging.

CHAPTER ONE

WHAT ARE YOU WILLING TO LOSE?

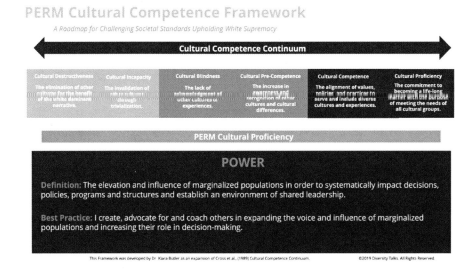

PERM Cultural Competence Framework

A Roadmap for Challenging Societal Standards Upholding White Supremacy

Cultural Competence Continuum

Cultural Destructiveness	Cultural Incapacity	Cultural Blindness	Cultural Pre-Competence	Cultural Competence	Cultural Proficiency
The elimination of other culture for the benefit of the white dominant narrative.	The invalidation of other cultures through trivialization.	The lack of acknowledgment of other cultures or experiences.	The increase in recognition of other cultures and cultural differences.	The alignment of values, policies, and practice to serve and include diverse cultures and experiences.	The commitment to becoming a life-long learner with the purpose of meeting the needs of all cultural groups.

PERM Cultural Proficiency

POWER

Definition: The elevation and influence of marginalized populations in order to systematically impact decisions, policies, programs and structures and establish an environment of shared leadership.

Best Practice: I create, advocate for and coach others in expanding the voice and influence of marginalized populations and increasing their role in decision-making.

This Framework was developed by Dr. Kiara Butler as an expansion of Cross et al., (1989) Cultural Competence Continuum. ©2019 Diversity Talks. All Rights Reserved.

CONTENT WARNING: This chapter explores themes around generational trauma, abuse, and addiction.

Terms and Conditions ('Terms')

The following terms will be used throughout this chapter. You may also notice the terms referenced in other chapters of this book. If you ever need a reminder of what a term means or the context in which it is used, review the full list of terms located at the end of the book.

Blaming: the act of wrongly accusing someone.

Bootstrap Ideology: the belief that hard work is the only determinant of success.

Economic Abuse: controlling a person's access by utilizing financial resources.

Emotional Abuse: verbal threats and behaviors that manipulate a person's decisions.

Denying: the act of refusing to admit the truth.

False Charity: the act of providing resources and opportunities to oppressed populations with the intention of helping them, while still preserving the power of the oppressor.

Marginalized: social, political, and economic exclusion or insignificance.

Microaggressions: verbal and/or environmental discriminatory behaviors that subtly communicate a prejudice towards a racial group.

Minimizing: the act of reducing.

Power: the elevation and influence of marginalized populations in order to systematically impact decisions, policies, programs and structures, and establish an environment of shared leadership.

Privilege: a special advantage, immunity, permission, right, or benefit granted to or enjoyed by an individual, class, or caste.

Societal Norms: rules that shape a person's values, actions, beliefs, and expectations for self and others.

White Supremacy: a culture that associates whiteness as ideal or superior by centralizing a white dominant narrative in systems, structures, and policies.

A Letter to My Stepfather

i've attempted to dissociate myself from what
you did to me so much that the fragments of
memories i have wouldn't be enough for a
substantial argument; they still aren't.

you molested me and when i do somehow
manage to trick myself into forgetting, my body
is the second-best record keeper.

i'm having a hard time finding the words to say
to you. it's most likely one of the reasons i've
never confronted you for what you did to me.

i blamed myself.
hated my inner being.
questioned my value.

i should have been smarter.
i should have told someone.
i should have confronted you.

but how would a child know to do this?
how would i know that it wasn't my fault?

my brain was too undeveloped then, but now it
is not. i don't think.

do you know how heavy that is for a child to carry?

i used to fear that you would use my incoherent sentences as a way to invalidate what i would say; my sentences are still incoherent as i'm trying to locate the words even now. and yet, here i am. the one who has to live with the trauma of her stepfather's actions. writing you this letter as if you deserve my words to meet pen to paper. the memories that i've blocked out...ones that i've chosen not to remember because of you. and still you're able to navigate this earth. this space. as if nothing ever happened.

there were days when i wanted to stop breathing.

do you know what that feels like? the feeling of suffocating?

for someone else to take your breath? your voice? the only thing you own? my body.

you took away my voice before i even knew how to use it. you snatched my thoughts. my confidence. my body.

i trusted you. i thought i was safe with you.

and i didn't even get to choose.

the life i'm living now.
how much you shaped it and are shaping it.
how much i have to remember.
the number of times that i have to remind
myself that it wasn't my fault.
even as i write this letter.

do you know what that feels like? the feeling of
guilt?

for something that was forced upon you.

you have a daughter.

you
    have
        a
           daughter.

those exact words repeat in my mind ever so
often. those exact words led me to believe that
i was one of them. i was not your daughter.

i prayed for you to die on most days, if not all
of them. i wanted the worst possible things to
happen to you.

the minutes that felt like hours.
the hours that felt like days.
day after day, year after year, you chipped
away at my innocence while navigating the

world as if the secret you asked me to keep
didn't exist.

Your Secret.

the persona you built that had everyone
fooled.

you bought me front row concert tickets to see
my favorite artists.
you gave me money for every "A" i got in
school.
you coerced me into playing the *games* that
were solely for your pleasure.
you assured me that you were preparing me
for my first kiss.
you asked for hugs only to end up on top of
me..

my childhood memories don't exist without the
latter.

how do you get to live?

how do you get to live your life?

how do you get to live your life with no
remorse?

how do you get to be...free?

Power

Definition: The elevation and influence of marginalized populations in order to systematically impact decisions, policies, programs and structures, and establish an environment of shared leadership.

Traditional power dynamics have distorted our views of safety, including how it looks and feels, which has resulted in complicating the shared responsibility it takes for individuals to experience safety. For generations, our society has granted people in positions of power authority, which has postured them to be saviors, decision makers, and the ideal standard.

As a former domestic violence educator, my work is heavily grounded in the cycle of abuse and tactics used by perpetrators to maintain power and control (Babcock et al., 1993). Essentially, it's the ability to recognize where people are within the cycle even when some are unaware that they are victims. I became interested in advocating for people who have survived domestic violence, sexual assault, and childhood trauma after grappling with the fact that I didn't have the voice, knowledge, or even resources to advocate for myself growing up.

I'm originally from the South and I definitely recall being taught to respect my elders.

"Listen when an adult is speaking to you."

"Don't talk back when you're being told something."

"Say yes ma'am and yes sir, or no ma'am and no sir to anyone older than you."

Respectability politics are instilled in households across the country but have a trickle effect on how we interact with others daily (Higginbotham, 1993). Ultimately, the learned behavior of not wanting to question authority, to not freely express opinions that go against the majority, to believe the masses when it comes to societal standards or ideals, even when the messages being received insult your existence, work to strip individuals of power.

That is the subtleness of living in a racist society.

While I was able to survive the abuse I experienced as a child, I now have to navigate living and surviving in the United States in unique but similar ways. Today, my lived experiences as a Black woman are largely invalidated or go unheard. I constantly have to work against societal stereotypes and anti-Blackness. And even while doing this work to change the narrative, blame is still placed on my entire race instead of the root cause, which is white supremacy.

Systemic oppression exists because of the societal need to position whiteness as the ideal or standard. We have accepted this as a norm. This positionality creates an interconnectedness between the cycle of abuse and systemic oppression through the exertion of power and control. Yet, cognitive dissonance has created space for us to collectively ignore the role we play as a society, which leaves a lasting impact that is twofold:

1.) An environment is created where those within positions of power continue to reinforce societal norms and messaging at the expense of others' identities.

2.) The victims within this dynamic begin to internalize the oppression experienced.

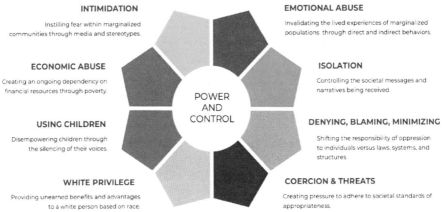

SYSTEMIC OPPRESSION

INTIMIDATION
Instilling fear within marginalized communities through media and stereotypes.

EMOTIONAL ABUSE
Invalidating the lived experiences of marginalized populations through direct and indirect behaviors.

ECONOMIC ABUSE
Creating an ongoing dependency on financial resources through poverty.

ISOLATION
Controlling the societal messages and narratives being received.

POWER AND CONTROL

USING CHILDREN
Disempowering children through the silencing of their voices.

DENYING, BLAMING, MINIMIZING
Shifting the responsibility of oppression to individuals versus laws, systems, and structures.

WHITE PRIVILEGE
Providing unearned benefits and advantages to a white person based on race.

COERCION & THREATS
Creating pressure to adhere to societal standards of appropriateness.

This power and control wheel through the lens of systemic oppression was adopted from the original resource created by the Domestic Abuse Intervention Project in 1984.

Denying, Blaming, & Minimizing

Black girls who are harmed or abused during childhood are less likely to report the abuse than their white counterparts. Statements such as "she wanted it to happen" or labels of being "fast" contribute to this lack of reporting. In the United States, adultification bias suggests that Black girls are less innocent, grow up quicker, and are more emotionally mature (Crenshaw, 1991). Unfortunately, such labels and categorization biases can lead to minimizing, denying, and blaming Black girls for their experiences even in instances where they aren't at fault.

Being falsely accused was one of the leading feelings I felt that caused me not to speak out about being molested. There were numerous times when the words would be at the tip of my tongue but then suddenly become overshadowed by how people would respond if I did decide to speak. I also didn't want to be judged or labeled as hyper-sexual.

As a society, we tend to label situations that we don't fully understand because it's easier to classify a situation or person based on their past experiences rather than grapple with the complexity of humanity. In retrospect, I shied away from the idea of people minimizing the abuse that I was experiencing whether intentionally or unintentionally due to the narratives we are typically exposed to about abuse and who is responsible.

"She wanted it to happen"

Countless findings show that the percentage of Black girls who report abuse is 6.7% (Crenshaw et al., 2015; Burke, 2017). It makes me pause when I think about the number of Black girls, like myself, who also felt powerless or too fearful to speak up and did not report. Notably, the blame that society places on victims feels traumatizing and, in some cases, has had a similar impact as the abuse itself. It seemed more manageable for me at the time not to relive the trauma associated with people repeatedly asking me accusatory questions.

I didn't want to take on that responsibility.

Systemic Oppression

In *Pedagogy of the Oppressed* (1970), Brazilian philosopher Paulo Freire discusses a phenomenon called false charity. What makes this idea of charity false is that even though efforts being made may rightfully help people who are in need, the efforts only address the symptom. We tend to do too much false charity work in the United States. One way that false charity functions is by providing resources and opportunities to oppressed populations with the intention of helping them while still allowing individuals in power to preserve their right to oppress. This preservation of power only benefits the power holders and as a result, those who seek or need liberation remain confined within a perpetual cycle of exploitation.

Indeed, the rise of the COVID-19 pandemic permitted the murders of Black people at the hands of the police to be amplified (Riggle et al., 2021). Since individuals were largely sheltering in place, time allowed people to bear witness, in unusual ways, to the ways in which Black people were losing their bodies and have lost their bodies at alarming rates. For instance, police body cam footage and cell phone recordings displayed on social media for public consumption exposed the number of unarmed Black people who have died in police custody. Yet, even with the sharing, the indictments or sentencing for those who committed such acts go unjustifiably unpunished more times than not. Fascinatingly, at the same time, we have increased our false charity work, while still controlling and accepting the societal narrative.

"But what about Black on Black crime?"

In the United States, we have accepted minimizing, denying, and blaming tactics typically identified in abusive power dynamics as a societal norm. When identifying the root cause for oppression in our country, it is easier to place blame on individuals rather than do the internal and collective work needed to dismantle systems of injustice.

Have you ever been in a room when someone asks the question, "But what about Black on Black crime?"

This framing of systemic oppression is intentionally focused on highlighting Black people, specifically Black men, who commit violent acts as criminals, with little focus on the systems and structures responsible for creating an environment where this exposure to violence is able to exist and thrive (Bell, 2003).

Comparative Law

The adultification of Black girls and the argument of Black on Black crime receive similar societal responses from authoritative figures who do not always share the same racial background. Within school settings, Black girls continue to receive disciplinary infractions at disproportionate rates in relation to their white peers. Research shows that Black girls are six times more likely to be unfairly disciplined for not adhering to the school dress code and receive harsher punishments in general, contributing to the over-criminalization of Black youth (Crenshaw et al., 2015). This racial comparison is also true for the imprisonment of Black adults who commit similar offenses as white adults.

Research shows that Black people are five times more likely to be incarcerated than white people (Wacquant, 2017). However, as a society, we have continuously **ignored**

narratives where whiteness affords privileges to those in its proximity, even if it is at the expense of someone else.

Emotional Abuse

There are a number of contributing factors as to whether or not a survivor of abuse remains silent. "Tell someone" or other recommendations for seeking help are common societal responses provided to survivors. Yet, in the United States, nine out of ten survivors do not report abusive behaviors and admiration has been identified as one of the reasons survivors of abuse don't speak out (Prochuk, 2018). In essence, prominence the abuser has within family or community structures may cause the abuse survivor to fear being disbelieved due to existing relationships built with the abuser.

My stepfather got really good at playing dual roles. I didn't recognize it at the time but now when I reflect back on his interactions with me when we were alone and compare them to his interactions with me when we were around family and friends, he wore the façade of the community hype man, a father, and an all-around good person. His duality led me to believe that people wouldn't address the abuse based on their perceptions and interactions with him. It also made me internalize the possibility that the abuse I was experiencing was imaginative.

"Tell someone."

As a child, I was unsure how to navigate this power dynamic or fear of preferential treatment. Essentially, telling someone didn't seem like an option. It seemed easier for me to stay silent than not to be believed.

Systemic Oppression

The Portuguese language has the incredible ability to encapsulate a concept or feeling in one word, which Freire does so aptly in *Pedagogy of the Oppressed*. He argues that in order to truly liberate the oppressed, we must seek to gain a level of social consciousness that allows us to reimagine rules, policies, and procedures that influence what we believe to be the status quo or normal—conscientização. We must seek the input and direction from those most impacted by oppressive systems; however, in the United States, voices of marginalized populations have been silenced in ways that may cause individuals to not recognize their power or not have access to language that articulates need. This is a result of an oppressive system operating as designed.

"When I look at you, I don't see color."

As a society, we have accepted emotional abuse tactics as a norm by continuously labeling microaggressions as well-intentioned actions. Microaggressions exist when a victim experiences verbal and/or environmental discriminatory behaviors that are subtle enough to be overlooked or dismissed (Pierce, 1970). A statement like "When I look at you, I don't see color," or an instance where a Black person is being followed around in a store are a few examples of how microaggressions do not explicitly translate to harm immediately even though the harm still exists. Ultimately, this ambiguity and indirect nature makes it hard to recognize or pinpoint this particular form of emotional abuse, which sometimes causes victims to question if the abuse is real.

Comparative Law

The lack of disclosure of abuse and the inability to identify and confront microaggressions may be due to the dominant societal response of an individual not being believed. When a person consistently receives messages that invalidate their lived experience, there is an increase in reluctance to go against the majority. Research shows that microaggressions are linked to low self-esteem and hopelessnesses (Pierce, 1970). This is also consistent with findings on the impact of emotional abuse tactics. Research shows that people who are victims of emotional abuse may experience learned helplessness as a result of feeling powerless (Prochuk, 2018). Comparatively speaking, both circumstances, being criticized, demeaned, or gaslit, are all actions that result in this outcome of powerlessness. However, as a society we have continuously **created environments where shame and hopelessness are processed inwardly by abuse survivors because those in positions of power are unwilling to take responsibility for their oppressive actions.**

Economic Abuse

Growing up, we watched and read a lot of fairytale stories of a damsel in distress who needed to be rescued by a knight in shiny armor. Oftentimes, the knight is rewarded for guiding the damsel to freedom even if it means that in the end, her freedom is determined by her reliance on her savior. In a sobering way, those false narratives of the damsel being saved rarely play out in abusive relationships. Instead, as a society we have become accustomed to Black women being in distress. This disguise, then, creates a perpetual cycle that forces those who experience abuse to shoulder the responsibility of saving themselves or passively waiting to be rescued.

"Why didn't you leave?"

Economic abuse is a tactic used by perpetrators to create a dynamic of reliance within a relationship. Within this dynamic, the survivor may feel a lack of autonomy over decisions made in terms of finances. Staggeringly, in the United States more than 90% of domestic violence survivors report experiencing behaviors that contribute to economic abuse (Follingstad et al., 1990). Statements like "Why didn't you leave?" disregard the imbalance in power that exists within these relationships and as a society, we have accepted this imbalance.

Growing up, parts of me unconsciously accepted the imbalance too. I thought that if I spoke up, my mother would be a *single mother* again, and she would have to navigate those complexities. So it seemed easier for me at the time not to break up the household she had built.

Systemic Oppression

Throughout my K-12 education experience, my lunch was free and to me that was freedom. What I realize now is that I was receiving free lunch in response to food insecurity, instead of the system addressing why students like myself didn't have access to high quality nutrition (Bowen et al., 2021). Many are still unaware that while free lunch programs are important, they are largely rooted in the lack of economic empowerment. In my innocence, I wasn't aware that I was being groomed to assimilate within an unjust system that positioned "free" as "freedom." I, and so many like me, were part of a system where the free, yet limited resources provided by the oppressor out of "good will," were disguised as freedom, which is often a false narrative created and maintained to keep people living in poverty.

"Just pull yourself up by your bootstraps."

Within the context of the United States, one way we have accepted economic abuse as a societal norm is through the ideology that poverty is a result of an individual's actions. The idea that a person is able to work themselves out of poverty and into a financially sustainable lifestyle or that individuals should "just pull themselves up by their bootstraps," borrowing from Booker T. Washington, regardless of our circumstances, disregards the policies, laws, and historical contexts that contribute to individuals and households living below the poverty line.

Comparative Law

Economic abuse and generational poverty continue to exist within our society due to a shared dependency of resources. Research shows that a person's inability to support themselves is one of the top reasons for staying in an abusive dynamic (Follingstad et al., 1990). This is a similar finding for households living below the poverty line. Research shows that government funded anti-poverty programs are less likely to increase economic independence through the building of generational wealth due to households being reliant on the programs at disproportionate rates (Harrison, 2004). For generations, households living below the poverty line have not been provided resources that put them at a competitive advantage and have instead been given only enough resources for those in positions to "check a box." However, as a society, we have continuously **accepted an outcome where those in positions of power do not address the social hierarchy that further reinforces dependency among oppressed groups.**

Fine Print

Having individual privileges that are considered a societal norm, may hinder us from acknowledging the fine print. Here are the key takeaways from Chapter 1:

Now that we've developed a common language and identified where we may be on the journey of relinquishing power and control, it is your turn to do the internal work. Using the Terms provided for this chapter and the Terms & Conditions Workbook page 1, respond to the reflection prompts in the space provided. When responding to the prompts, keep in mind that there is no correct or incorrect answer.

CHAPTER TWO

CAN MULTIPLE NARRATIVES EXIST?

Before beginning this chapter, ensure you've completed the anti-racist work required in the Power dimension. The journey of incorporating anti-racist best practices is not a linear one. It is also not a race. You may find the need to revisit a chapter or even add to your responses in the accompanying workbook. There is no finish line or time constraint in completing this book.

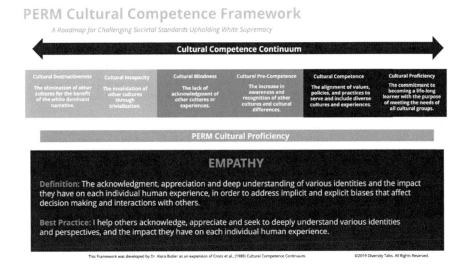

PERM Cultural Competence Framework

A Roadmap for Challenging Societal Standards Upholding White Supremacy

Cultural Competence Continuum

Cultural Destructiveness	Cultural Incapacity	Cultural Blindness	Cultural Pre-Competence	Cultural Competence	Cultural Proficiency
The elimination of other cultures for the benefit of the white dominant narrative.	The invalidation of other cultures through trivialization.	The lack of acknowledgment of other cultures or experiences.	The increase in awareness and recognition of other cultures and cultural differences.	The alignment of values, policies, and practices to serve and include diverse cultures and experiences.	The commitment to becoming a life-long learner with the purpose of meeting the needs of all cultural groups.

PERM Cultural Proficiency

EMPATHY

Definition: The acknowledgment, appreciation and deep understanding of various identities and the impact they have on each individual human experience, in order to address implicit and explicit biases that affect decision making and interactions with others.

Best Practice: I help others acknowledge, appreciate and seek to deeply understand various identities and perspectives, and the impact they have on each individual human experience.

This Framework was developed by Dr. Kiara Butler as an expansion of Cross et al. (1989) Cultural Competence Continuum. ©2019 Diversity Talks. All Rights Reserved.

CONTENT WARNING: This chapter explores themes around generational trauma, abuse, and addiction.

Terms and Conditions ('Terms')

The following terms will be used throughout this chapter.

Core Identity: the core identity comprises an individual's intersecting identities, experiences, values, and beliefs. It is the most central aspect of an individual's being and is often referred to as "what makes you, you."

Examples: race, gender identity, gender expression, sexual orientation, socio-economic status, ability status, etc.

Empathy: the acknowledgment, appreciation and deep understanding of various identities and their impact on each individual human experience, to address implicit and explicit biases that affect decision-making and interactions with others.

False Empathy: the ability to understand another person's experiences or circumstances without relinquishing power and control.

Intersectionality: the interconnected nature of social categorizations such as race, class, and gender as they apply to a given individual or group, regarded as creating overlapping and interdependent systems of discrimination or disadvantage.

Implicit Bias: the attitudes or stereotypes that unconsciously affect our understanding, actions, and decisions.

Narrative Resiliency: the prioritization of perseverance based on societal standards of strength.

Perspective Taking: the willingness to mitigate bias by seeking to understand another person's experience or circumstances.

Sympathy: to feel bad or apologetic for the circumstances or experiences of others.

A Letter to My Mother

I still remember when he first touched me.
I still smell the room.
I see it.

The maroon and gold comforter and decor. It's
a reminder of my stolen innocence.

A reminder of my guilt.

Each day he took advantage of me and each
day I woke up thinking it was my fault.

I waited for you to get home from work on
most days, if not all of them. I hoped that there
wasn't traffic or you didn't stop at the store so
that you would make it home at 5:25 pm to
save me from him. Your husband.

I needed you to release me from the toxic and
damaging routine that he created with me.

"Come home and do your homework," you said.
*"Alton will let you know when you can get on
the phone."*

Little did you know, the phone was the only
thing that saved me from him when you
weren't home. It was my only escape until you
showed up like clockwork. When I heard the

sound of the garage going up, I sighed with relief because it symbolized that I had made it through another day.

I survived only until the next morning.

Only until tomorrow when my footsteps met the pavement as I ran home from the bus.

I still think about why I would run home and what I was running to. Was it a home that lacked protection? Was it a home where I wasn't seen? Where my pain or my scars went unknown? Maybe it was the home where I had mistaken my stepfather's touch for love. I really don't know.

but ...

How did you not know?
How did you not see the signs?
Where was your intuition?

You know what I'm talking about, too.
The one where they say mothers always know when something is wrong with their child.
Your husband molested me for years, and you didn't notice. And if your intuition wasn't enough, the words from my mouth weren't either. At least, not in the way that I thought they would be. I thought that you would have

believed me, but his presence still lingered for years, even after you knew.

He still stayed with us and played the role of a stepfather.

You still shared space,
slept in the same bed,
went on dates,
family trips,
and shared all the other intimate moments
with him because you were lovers.

Was receiving his love that important to you?
More important than the love of your
daughter?
My love?
It felt that way.

Did you think that if you ignored it long
enough it would go away?

All those years that went by and you never
even mentioned it. And so, I didn't mention it.

To anyone.

I didn't think I was supposed to.

I was following your lead.

The lead of my mother, and you never even checked on me or considered asking how I was or how I was coping. I thought we were in this together. I thought that I was your everything. I needed you and I feel my only lifeline did nothing.

Even after all the swimming lessons.
The proactive measures you took in warning me about adulthood.
I really feel like you "put your mask on first before assisting others."
Me.

You let me drown.

And all of these years, I've carried rage and suppressed my feelings because I was afraid to hurt yours. So instead, I continuously hurt myself. I learned to stay silent. To people please. To not cause too much attention. All because I was afraid to break up the home you built and found comfort in, even at the expense of my own sanity. Even if it meant me not feeling like a part of it.

To be honest, sometimes I still don't.
You would think me moving halfway across the country would make me miss home.
That I would crave to be around family.
The familiarity.
The southern comfort foods.

But when I think of home, I only think of being malnourished.
And so, I will no longer eat the words that you deserve to hear.
It's not worth the agony.
And it's not mine to hold.

I release this trauma from my body.
I release this pain.
I release this guilt.
I release the feeling of abandonment.
I release the feeling of resentment towards you and towards myself.

I vow that if I ever have children, I will protect *them* with my heart, my soul, and my physical being.

I vow to never be you.

Empathy

Definition: The acknowledgment, appreciation and deep understanding of various identities and their impact on each individual human experience, to address implicit and explicit biases that affect decision-making and interactions with others.

When I consider all the ways in which I'm empathetic towards other people, I often question if I allow or even know how to accept another person's expression of empathy towards me. For some reason, I have believed that receiving compassion was a form of pity or that it meant someone better off than me, regardless of the circumstance, was looking to console me. The person couldn't possibly understand or know what I'm feeling.

Navigating spaces and experiences as a woman, not to mention a Black woman, comes with societal pressures. Indeed, society places unrealistic expectations on women that force us to perform strength in unhealthy ways (Harris, 2002). For instance, women in business are expected not to show emotion for fear of being considered weak. If you consider the core identity of being Black and how those two identities intersect, there is an added expectation of resilience. Kimberlé Crenshaw (1989) believes that it is crucial to acknowledge the uniqueness of our identities and how they influence our experiences. Unfortunately, society has brainwashed Black women to think that our pain isn't as painful as the next person's and that our strength keeps us *useful*. I use the word *useful* because the Black woman is the lowest on the totem pole in American society.

I can hear the fear of rejection cracking in my bones.

I can feel the embarrassment of being weak coursing through my veins.

The weight of the world sitting on my shoulders with her feet crossed, creating the illusion that resilience is the answer.

This narrative of resiliency and other beliefs inspired by racialized social stereotypes got us here; to the place where vulnerability and the expression of emotions are frowned upon, which causes us to suppress those feelings (Allen et al., 2019). To the place where false empathy continues to thrive because we haven't done the internal reflections required to truly understand what it means to put yourself in another person's position without corrupting the situation with bias.

That is the subtleness of living in a racist society.

This distorted reality of strength and resilience takes form in different ways. For some, it may inhibit our ability to conceptualize the actions of others if they contradict or are not similar to our own. It may cause them to avoid engaging in dialogue that others could view as confrontational.

Authentic empathy is the acknowledgment, appreciation, and deep understanding of various identities and their impact on each human experience. It is rooted in the need to address implicit and explicit biases that affect decision-making and interactions with others (Diversity Talks, 2017). Yet, it is the deep understanding part that is most complex. We can seek to understand someone's experiences and life views at the surface while simultaneously holding space within ourselves to refute their experiences with the word "but." Even if we don't express this feeling of hesitancy or reluctance out loud, our subconscious makes a note and subtly forms a separate reality around this belief.

Moreover, to have a deep understanding of something requires that you let go of your reality and submit to someone else's reality. Piaget (1992) defines this approach as perspective taking. Honestly, this part of the work is easier said than done, which is why most of our interactions with other people are sympathetic. However, creating a world where multiple narratives exist even if they contradict each other, even if it's "not something you would do," requires the release of power and control and openness to the possibility of being hurt.

REMINDER

Revisit Chapter 1 Fine Print on page 43 and your personal reflections on the importance of relinquishing power and control. Come back to this section when you are grounded in where you are on your journey within the Power dimension.

After writing and sending the letter to my mother, I reached out **to have a conversation**—the conversation that we had avoided for what felt like centuries. To carry something so heavy in my body for so long wore on me, but it also ashamedly became my armor in the same instance. I think back to moments when I was growing up, in the early 2000s to be exact. Erykah Badu's song "Bag Lady" would come on the radio, and I would sing it wondering why a person would carry so. many. bags. to. a. bus. stop. Full stop. Yet, that unsound logic didn't stop me from singing along in falsetto *"pack light."* I giggle on the inside now as an adult when I hear the song acknowledging my youthful ignorance and fleeting innocence.

And a reminder that my mother had her own bags.

I wrote *A Letter to My Mother* as a way to process the emotions I had suppressed since I was eight years old. I needed to work through the person I had made her out to be all those years. I also wanted **to understand better her perspective** on navigating raising three young Black girls in Mississippi as a single parent. I can't imagine the pain she must've carried from experiencing a divorce, accompanied by the pressure of securing income sufficient to care for my sisters and me. She must've also felt the guilt of not being able to be everywhere and everything to everyone.

"I still contemplate why I would run home. What was I running to? A home that lacked protection. A home that didn't see me, my pain, or my scars."

I wrote *A Letter to My Mother* **to release what I had perceived to be her reality. To ask the questions** that had gone unanswered, the questions that I felt she ignored.

*"How did you not know?
How did you not see the signs?
Where was your intuition?"*

Earlier in the chapter, I provided examples of how societal pressures impact how Black women process and respond to situations. But, I admit, my emotional attachment to the narrative I constructed about my mother wouldn't allow me to apply those same societal pressures to this experience. Indeed, it was much easier for me to place blame on her and center myself as the hero in my own search for rescue.

Writing this chapter made me wonder how often we do not consider the circumstances of other people because of our emotional ties to the situation. Or even because of our attachment to a narrative that positions us as the victim and not the villain. Engaging in this perspective-taking process with my mother required me **to focus less on self-preservation and protection** and even the need to be right.

Zaretta Hammond (2015) describes this feeling as a common reaction when our social interactions activate what the brain perceives as threats imposed by implicit bias. Our biases, which no one is immune to, can cause us to go into fight or flight mode. It can also cause us to freeze. If I am honest, those emotions—the feelings of fear, anger, and guilt—still rightfully surface for me today as my mother and I engage in dialogue, but it was through this process that I am now able to unpack how this one experience is being carried and felt by both of us. I am grateful that I can now pinpoint how the repercussions of our actions influence our day-to-day interactions with others, even if it's on a subconscious level.

Ultimately, the relationship with my mother serves as my roadmap for authentic empathy. As you can see, I didn't choose a situation that I could easily separate from myself. In fact, I chose a situation that I will have to continue working at for years to come because I will have to continue strengthening the muscle that will allow me to take my assumptions and beliefs out of the situation to fully embrace my mother's reality. I must do the work, though, even if it is at the risk of me repeating the perpetual cycle of reluctance, leaving no one to hold liable for the repercussions but myself.

Disclaimer: Empathy Best Practices

Engage in dialogue to gain insight into the perspective of another person.
Seek a better understanding without invalidating a person's experience.
Release the need to control or manipulate the narrative.
Ask questions to gain clarity.
Focus less on self-preservation and protection.

Fine Print

Sometimes our inability to be vulnerable or fear of being hurt, may cloud our judgment, hindering us from acknowledging the fine print. Here are the key takeaways from Chapter 2:

scan me for fine print

Now that we've developed a common language and identified where we may be on the journey of expressing authentic empathy, it is your turn to do the internal work. Using the Terms provided for this chapter and the Terms & Conditions Workbook page 10, respond to the reflection prompts in the space provided. When responding to the prompts, keep in mind that there is no correct or incorrect answer.

CHAPTER THREE

ARE YOU REALLY WELL?

Before beginning this chapter, ensure you've completed the anti-racist work required in the Empathy dimension. The journey of incorporating anti-racist best practices is not a linear one. It is also not a race. You may find the need to revisit a chapter or even add to your responses in the accompanying workbook. There is no finish line or time constraint in completing this book.

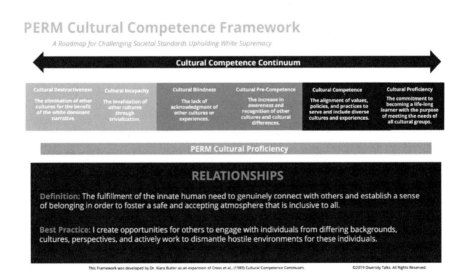

PERM Cultural Competence Framework
A Roadmap for Challenging Societal Standards Upholding White Supremacy

Cultural Competence Continuum

Cultural Destructiveness	Cultural Incapacity	Cultural Blindness	Cultural Pre-Competence	Cultural Competence	Cultural Proficiency
The elimination of other cultures for the benefit of the white dominant narrative.	The invalidation of other cultures through trivialization.	The lack of acknowledgment of other cultures or experiences.	The increase in awareness and recognition of other cultures and cultural differences.	The alignment of values, policies, and practices to serve and include diverse cultures and experiences.	The commitment to becoming a life-long learner with the purpose of meeting the needs of all cultural groups.

PERM Cultural Proficiency

RELATIONSHIPS

Definition: The fulfillment of the innate human need to genuinely connect with others and establish a sense of belonging in order to foster a safe and accepting atmosphere that is inclusive to all.

Best Practice: I create opportunities for others to engage with individuals from differing backgrounds, cultures, perspectives, and actively work to dismantle hostile environments for these individuals.

This Framework was developed by Dr. Kiara Butler as an expansion of Cross et al., (1989) Cultural Competence Continuum. ©2019 Diversity Talks. All Rights Reserved.

CONTENT WARNING: This chapter explores themes around generational trauma, abuse, and addiction.

Terms and Conditions ('Terms')

The following terms will be used throughout this chapter.

Abandonment: the act of leaving a person, place, or thing for an indefinite period.

Anti-Blackness: prejudice behaviors, assumptions, or beliefs held against Black people.

Cognitive Dissonance: conflicting or inconsistent attitudes, behaviors, and beliefs.

Fictive Kinship: a significant relationship built through social ties.

Patriarchy: the prioritization of masculinity within society.

Relationships: the fulfillment of the innate human need to genuinely connect with others and establish a sense of belonging in order to foster a safe and accepting atmosphere that is inclusive to all.

Self-Reliance: an individual's ability to sustain on their own.

Toxic Masculinity: societal pressures for how manhood should look.

Vulnerability: an openness to being exposed
to harm.

A Letter to My Father

Growing up, I longed for you most days, if not all of them.
I wanted the protection and the comfort that I heard a dad provides.
I never got the chance to know how a father's love felt.
You weren't there to teach me how to ride a bike, adjust the seat if it was too high, or to take my training wheels off. As a result, you missed the time I scrapcd my knee, and man, do I still have the scar to prove it.

I went through my first heartbreak alone in the 5th grade, and I thought my world was ending. I remember I played sad love songs on repeat for months, and you would have thought that I had a clear grasp of what love was. But I did not.

You missed my first kiss.
First school dance.
Parent-teacher conferences.
Track meets.

You missed football games where I was a cheerleader. I remember the subtle waves my cheer mates received from their parents that I would humbly ignore. I remember, but you don't.
Prom. Missed.

Graduation. All 6 of them. Elementary school, middle school, high school, undergrad, master's, and my doctoral one. Missed. I think I finally got the hint around undergrad. It was the very last ticket I sent for you to come.

I had to experience so many of life's precious and not so precious moments without you. I needed you.
I learned how to drive a car without you, and I had to figure out all of the *manly* things society says I'm supposed to learn from my dad, like how to work a power drill or jumpstart a car. I figured those things out by myself (and YouTube). Alone.

I guess what I'm trying to say is that I had to because you didn't provide me with a choice.

Yet still, the ghost of you haunts me. The lingering memories of our handful of interactions. The questions that have gone unanswered.

I often look in the mirror, and staring back at me is a reflection of you.

There's a saying, "*you don't get to choose your parents,*" and I'm reminded of that saying each time I catch a glimpse of the patch of curly gray strands of hair positioned at the front of my crown.

Just like yours.

... or my brown button nose, the dimples at the bottom of my cheeks that surface each time I feel the slightest bit of happiness.

Just like yours.

I am yours.

I laughed the other day; it was one of those belly laughs and if I didn't know any better, I could have mistaken the noise parting my lips as yours.

I often look at you in the mirror, and I try to recall the sound of your voice.

There's a saying, *"you don't get to choose your parents,"* and I guess the part missing from this statement is that you don't get to choose their presence either. I had to grow up with just a projection of you. Even as I... we get older, the idea of having a father only lives in my mind.

Sadly, I've mourned your death more than a thousand times, and I have to admit that it's

more painful to grieve a person when they are
still alive.

How can I miss someone I never knew?
How can I long for my phone to ring and a
stranger is on the other end?

I have so much to tell you. So much that
you've missed.

I made it out of the Jacktown streets. I learned
how to tie my own tie (yes, I wear ties and
bowties often). I started my own multi-million-
dollar company. I earned a doctorate. I bought
my first house.

But instead, my phone will never ring. My life
will keep moving forward without you, and
that little girl you may remember will continue
to long for you.

I look for you in the mirror often.

Relationships

Definition: The fulfillment of the innate human need to genuinely connect with others and establish a sense of belonging in order to foster a safe and accepting atmosphere that is inclusive to all.

No one ever really mentions how the impact of your childhood relationships, or the lack thereof, manifests in adulthood. While we establish most of our relationships through connection, how we view connection may be based on our witnessed relationships on various levels. I didn't learn what the word abandonment actually meant until I grew older, though I experienced it my whole life. Moreover, I am confident that my body responded to the historical trauma I experienced even when I was not cognizant. Indeed, trauma is nuanced, and studies have shown that the body keeps the score. Fascinatingly, the body recognizes trauma before the human mind can grapple with its existence and before we're able to realize that we've been living in survival mode. Essentially, we are subconsciously protecting ourselves. Coping.

Unfortunately, I learned to cope unhealthily with not having a father around ten. There were weekends where we were supposed to spend time together that he missed. There were birthdays or holidays when I didn't receive a phone call.

There were arguments that I would overhear between my mother and him. There were legal battles where I was the liability.

And I still am.

Even at the age of thirty-two, I still don't have an answer as to why my two sisters and I weren't his chosen family and in that same breath of questioning, I can trace the pattern of longing to be chosen in most, if not all my relationships. Whether in romantic or platonic relationships, I accepted what was given to me, even if it meant remaining in toxic dynamics or not choosing myself. It was effortless for me to embrace not having my needs met.

Generally, we base genuine relationships on an individual's ability to meet other people's needs. In culture, many refer to this as the concept of pouring into another's cup while they pour into yours. The dual pouring allows people to feel a sense of belonging, which we all need to feel accepted and included in society (Diversity Talks, 2017). However, when we conceptualize relationships, we often miss the importance of providing to others based on their needs and not our own (Chapman, 2010). My father clearly lacked this concept and under certain circumstances, we all do.

To establish a genuine relationship with others, we must first be knowledgeable of our needs in order to express them to other people. As a collective, we tend to gravitate towards people who share the same identities as us, which reinforces a sense of fictive kinship. While we value like-mindedness, building relationships with people based on surface-level connections does not create space for us to consider others' perspectives and experiences, especially if they are different from our own. Unfortunately, this thought process instead builds false narratives around how belonging and inclusion will look.

"How did we as a society become so comfortable with not living our truths? Daily we're asked, "how we're doing" by our peers, colleagues or family and without even thinking, we utter the words "I'm well." But are you really well? 24 hours a day. 7 days a week. When is it okay to be humble enough to break down and say that life sucks today?"

TEDX2017

To establish a genuine relationship with others requires a level of vulnerability that goes beneath the surface. Yet, society has conditioned us to view vulnerability as a sign of weakness. Even in moments of confrontation or disagreement, we shy away from the vulnerable parts of ourselves, and instead, we channel feelings of hurt into anger. This is a learned behavior. We live in a society where patriarchy and toxic masculinity have conditioned us to want to achieve power and control in our day-to-day interactions. A society where patriarchy and toxic masculinity reap the benefits of male dominance while our relationships with others suffer because we've been taught to prioritize self-reliance, which is a trauma response.

My father was... is... an alcoholic. I believe that is where he found his self-reliance. There were days when he would call my phone around 8:00 pm every night, and sometimes I would answer because I missed his presence. He would call with just enough time to get his first sip of alcohol to send him back to the intoxication level from the night before. His speech was often slurred, which annoyed me because I couldn't figure out what he was trying to communicate. As years progressed, the annoyance was why I stopped answering the phone. As a result, the calls lessened but continued randomly at times.

One day they just stopped, and now his voice is only a collection of memories.

I believe my father relied on alcoholism as a way to cope. I still, to this day, have no clue what he was dealing with, though. Growing up it was rare to see him express his emotions, and that is something I crave now as an adult. I want to know the feeling of knowing my father's hurt and pain, and his happiness and love. But unfortunately, my childhood was absent of my father's love and protection.

Societal Messaging & Norms

"There's a saying, "you don't get to choose your parents" and I guess the part that is missing from this statement is that you don't get to choose their presence either."

Unfortunately, our society supports the single story of single-parent households from a deficit perspective, especially in Black households. We've been taught that Black homes lack family values or that the children will end up just like their parents. There are also a lot of false narratives about Black fathers and how fatherhood in Black households looks. Society tells us that all Black men will make babies and then leave without caring for them. We watch the news where headlines highlight Black men as criminals. When we hear these stories the blame is often placed on the individual (e.g., the father) without closely examining the system upholding the narratives and behaviors. For instance, Black men face challenges navigating society, and what Black fathers face while protecting their households figuratively and literally goes unnoticed.

Did my father internalize the societal narrative of Black men as deadbeat dads?

Did he allow toxic masculinity to prevent him from expressing his feelings?

I don't ask these questions to excuse my father for not being present in my life, but as a way of reflecting on the content from Chapter 2: "Can Multiple Narratives Exist?" Ultimately, I raise the questions considering his side of the story– the societal impact.

That is the subtleness of living in a racist society.

It's easy to overlook the complexities of individual relationships and how society influences these relationships, which is another example of us accepting what has been deemed the norm in forming connections. Largely, systemic oppression affects our ability to connect with others, intentionally or unintentionally. But because we form relationships on the micro-level, there is a disconnect between relationship building and macro-level outcomes. As a result, we are restricted in our ability to rightly view a situation from another person's perspective and are often limited in our ability to take action as a collective (Piaget, 1992). Overwhelmingly, we have collectively accepted segregation based on our identities as an established norm when building relationships, even when integration is a societal belief that all *good* people try to live up to. It is one of the reasons that when confronted about prejudiced acts and other discriminatory behaviors, white people tend to use the phrase "But I have Black friends" as a way to position themselves as a good person. However, this statement also ignores the impact of the person on the receiving end, the Black friend. There is still a lack of ownership of the discriminatory acts and discriminatory behaviors that no one is immune from (Greenwald & Banaji, 1995). There is a clear separation from Blackness up until it is beneficial.

> *"Racism exists but there is no way I can be racist,"* they said.

Considering the critical takeaways from
Chapter 1: "What Are You Willing to Lose?", we
can see how the aforementioned statements
are dangerous to us as a society but
specifically to marginalized groups. First, there
is a lack of ownership over the systems that
racism operates and thrives within and also
the impact. Sometimes the attempt to separate
the self from racism is made unknowingly, but
this is the same cognitive dissonance at the
root of all our interpersonal connections. For
instance, segregated schools, workplaces, and
housing are continuously reinforced through
our behaviors and the narratives we've created
as a society. These narratives don't just end at
a societal level, though; they also trickle back
into the micro-level: our households, personal
lives, and relationships through implicit and
explicit bias (Greenwald & Banaji, 1995).

Fine Print

Sometimes not experiencing the fulfillment of our innate human needs, may hinder us from acknowledging the fine print. Here are the key takeaways from Chapter 3:

scan me for fine print

Now that we've developed a common language and identified where we may be on the journey of establishing genuine relationships, it is your turn to do the internal work. Using the Terms provided for this chapter and the Terms & Conditions Workbook page 18, respond to the reflection prompts in the space provided. When responding to the prompts, keep in mind that there is no correct or incorrect answer.

CHAPTER FOUR

AT WHOSE EXPENSE?

Before beginning this chapter, ensure you've completed the anti-racist work required in the Relationships dimension. The journey of incorporating anti-racist best practices is not a linear one. It is also not a race. You may find the need to revisit a chapter or even add to your responses in the accompanying workbook. There is no finish line or time constraint in completing this book.

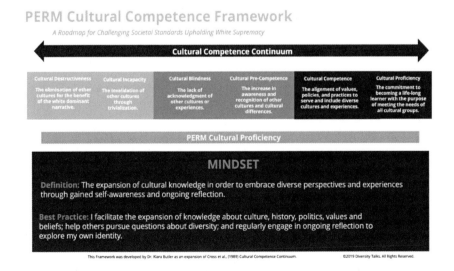

CONTENT WARNING: This chapter explores themes around generational trauma, abuse, and addiction.

Terms and Conditions ('Terms')

The following terms will be used throughout this chapter.

Abandonment: the act of leaving a person, place, or thing for an indefinite period.

Abomination: an act of disgrace.

American Dream: an equal opportunity provided to achieve success within the United States.

Internalized Oppression: beliefs in negative stereotypes and messaging based on the oppression a person may have experienced firsthand.

Mindset: the expansion of cultural knowledge in order to embrace diverse perspectives and experiences through gained self-awareness and ongoing reflection.

Opportunity Gap: opportunities afforded to a person based on their race, socio-economic status, or zip-code.

White Dominant Narrative: messaging that centers whiteness as the norm, causing others to change their behaviors to fit white standards of appropriateness.

White Fragility: a term used to describe the disbelieving defensiveness, discomfort, anger, or any strong emotions a white person experiences when their ideas about race or racism are challenged.

White Supremacy: a culture that associates whiteness as ideal or superior by centralizing a white dominant narrative in systems, structures, and policies.

A Letter to Myself

Younger self,

I'm sorry I didn't know how to love you.
To the point that I wouldn't even know what
love was... is now... if it were knocking at my
door.

The compromising. The comparison.
I'm sorry it took me so long to find you. So long
that I, too, still share the sudden feelings of
abandonment with you.

I'm sorry I didn't know how to parent you as I
watched you struggle to nurture yourself. I
didn't anticipate this as something I would be
expected to do.

I wanted to run away from you, from me, on
most days, if not all of them. To seek refuge in
a reality other than my own. Do you remember
the mornings when getting out of bed seemed
like the third hardest task? I remember staying
alive being the first and having to take care of
you, for me, the second.

Kiara, I'm sorry that I couldn't take care of
you. I didn't know how to choose you over
everything and everyone else who seemed more
important. I was never taught this skill.

You've wanted for as long as I can remember to
be chosen.
For people to see your value...
your worth,
your charisma,
your humor,
your sadness,
your pain,
your tears... you.

You've wanted for as long as I can remember
for people to see you. And I, the only person
you had left, didn't even recognize your worth.
I caused you to look for love and home in other
people, even those who weren't good for you.

I'm sorry that protecting you didn't look or feel
like it was supposed to. I thought that
protection meant making sacrifices, even if I
was sacrificing us.

I'm sorry that the things you needed as a child
felt so foreign.

The same as the voice you're hearing now as
you silently read this letter is a voice that no
longer sounds like home. The enunciation of
every syllable is my attempt to make sure that
you don't have to repeat yourself. The voice
that people compliment you on and make

statements like "you speak so eloquently," or
"you don't sound like you're from Mississippi."

I should've spoken up for you in those
moments. If I had, you wouldn't have
had to shape-shift to hide parts of yourself.
to suppress your feelings for other people's
comfort.

The guilt you had to hold that wasn't yours to
hold.
Your anger,
and rage,
and feelings of resentment.

And so, younger Kiara, I can see now how hard
it is to determine which voice you're hearing is
yours.

Don't listen to:

The southern voices whispering that you're an
abomination because of who you love.

The societal voices that apply unrealistic
pressures to achieve the American Dream.

The white voices yelling that your Blackness
isn't welcomed here even in 2022.

Their sounds simultaneously get louder,
mirroring rushing waves during a tsunami.

It is through those sounds that I hope you hear my voice. The voice silently speaking to you right now.

You, my dear, are enough.

Mindset

Definition: The expansion of cultural knowledge in order to embrace diverse perspectives and experiences through gained self-awareness and ongoing reflection.

I was reading Ta-Nehisi Coates's *Between the World and Me* (2015), and I was drawn to how he constructs the book to speak to his 15-year-old son through letter form, and I imagined how different my life would be if I had known when I was younger what I know now: that the Terms & Conditions of our society will not benefit the oppressed or the marginalized. I'm originally from Jackson, Mississippi, a small but mighty capital city with a predominantly Black population. So that means growing up, my mayor was Black, my superintendent was Black, and all of my teachers were Black. I had the privilege of maintaining that narrative through college because I attended Tougaloo College, a Historically Black College and University (HBCU).

It wasn't until I went off after undergrad that I realized how complex systems of oppression actually are. While I knew that systems of oppression existed on the surface, I wasn't really aware of how deep we internalize the oppression we experience, and through this internalization we may oppress other people within the varying systems that we are trying to overcome (Jr., 1992).

...and through this internalization, we may oppress other people within the varying systems that we are trying to overcome.

"The southern voices whispering that you're an abomination because of who you love."

Mississippi has shaped my life in several positive and negative ways. I grappled heavily with my sexual orientation and gender expression at a very early age in every space I occupied. Unfortunately, we live in a heteronormative world, so it may be hard to recognize this established norm if the images and messages you receive from society mirror your reality. But it isn't hard to miss someone who is queer or identifies as a part of the LGBTQ+ community, and their inner being craves the total opposite of what the majority feels is *right*.

Overwhelmingly, society teaches individuals that men and women are only supposed to share intimate relationships, especially in the Bible belt states. In addition, some commercials and movies primarily feature white men and white women falling in love, purchasing their first home, running with their kids in a big backyard, and obtaining the

American Dream as if Black people do not have similar experiences and desires. What is being pushed by these imaginary images are limited views of happiness, which function to ostracize individuals who do not fit within the confines of that single story.

Imagine being in elementary school, which is when many begin to form relationships, and suddenly realize that all connections aren't deemed appropriate by society or even those closest to you. I was a kid with big emotions, and I liked to express myself through my hairstyles and clothing. I also expressed my bigness through the eye-rolls and attitudes I would give my teachers even if they didn't deserve it. In retrospect, expression and the ability to express myself were really important for me, and I couldn't understand then, as my younger self, why the parts that I wanted to express growing up in

"Just like I didn't tell anyone that I was gay until my freshman year of college. It took a while for me to accept it myself because I wanted so badly to be straight. I would pray every night for me to no longer feel what I was feeling... for God to fix me and make my life like everyone else's. I would pray so much that my prayers had prayers."

TEDX2017

86

the 90s made me such a *bad* person.

Have you ever googled the word abomination?

If not, words like disgust, hatred, curse, horror, and disgrace are provided as synonyms. Imagine me as a child asking Jeeves, *"What is an abomination?"* and being provided with the synonyms. At that point, I realized that most, if not all, of the adults around me were using this word to describe me. While I didn't grow up in the church because the church wasn't something my mother made us attend every Thursday or Sunday like some of my friends, to live in the South is to live in a church.

"Growing up, I felt obligated to have a boyfriend because that's what everyone asked about. I can still remember at a very young age being questioned about what little boy I was crushing on in class. It was the favorite question that my grandmother and great aunt would ask every weekend. Other than my great aunt asking, "how's your hammer hanging?" and me still to this day, not having a clue what she was talking about. I would say a random name like Jeffrey or Adam, but in reality, my soul was crying out for me to say the girl's name that I would

constantly smile at, and she would smile back."

TEDX2017

I still have recollections of sitting in the backseat of my mother's car and seeing billboards warning us of Jesus' return as we drove throughout the state. The reminders were surrounded by red and orange flames warning that you should repent, be saved, or be banished to hell. People also held conversations around me, sharing old wives' tales of how hell feels, looks, and sounds. Wrapped in these tales and the voices in which individuals spoke was fear, which caused their voices to drop to a whisper when the word "*devil*" parted someone's lips.

I admit that I carried that fear with me everywhere I went. Every day of my existence, I thought that I was living only for God to sentence me to hell, but I couldn't find any logical reason why a God of love, grace, and forgiveness

"So, I went through my adolescent years seeking love from guys because that's what I thought I was supposed to do. I knew that if I were to come out and say that I was gay, I would have either been bullied or called an

would create someone as sinful as myself.

abomination or both. And so, I told no one."

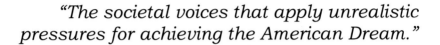

TEDX2017

"The societal voices that apply unrealistic pressures for achieving the American Dream."

After graduating undergrad, I made it out of what some people would consider the hood, and I was on a search to claim the riches that society had promised to me. I searched and searched for the American dream the United States claims to provide, only to experience homelessness for 365 days. I found myself sleeping on the floors of my closest friends and in the car, which was my only possession. My debt consumed me in ways that I didn't think were possible at those moments. This shouldn't have happened to me, especially not since people were praising me for having a degree that would surely "pay for itself."

Due to what felt like the voices from my past closing in on me and the societal pressure that I was experiencing, I sought refuge in addictions to numb the feelings of being queer, Black, and a woman in the United States. At the same time, I still felt every bit of resentment towards a system that society didn't build for me but that I operated within. It is no secret that the Terms & Conditions of our society benefit who they are supposed to. It prioritizes the needs and experiences of white people. People whose identities are in proximity to the dominant white narrative. People with the power to continuously propose and pass laws on behalf of everyone. People with privilege. With my degrees and other accolades, I somehow thought I was different in my naivete. I had worked hard as society told me to.

In *Between the World and Me*, Coates also delves into what it means to be Black in the United States and the struggle that we, as Black people, face when trying to achieve what society considers the American Dream. Embedded in the words that I shared in *A Letter to Myself*, the American Dream almost took my life and threatens to take the lives of so many people like

"It wasn't until I joined the education sector that I realized society has already placed the marker of failure on "low-income" students and I was one of them. I went through my adolescent years thinking that youth of color were given the same resources as everyone else. I didn't know that there were systems and structures in place that contributed and promoted the failures of entire races."

me. In the past, I
was trying to live up

TEDX2017

to the abstract expectation of *success,* who
obtains it, or the timeframe of when it is
achieved, and it left me defeated and
constricted by societal norms.

I learned and am continuing to learn that
survival presents itself differently depending
on an individual's circumstances. Therefore,
we must not assume that just because some
people are capable of surviving, we all have an
equal playing field to do so (Coates, 2015). It is
not surprising, then, that this very notion will
encourage many to ignore systems of
oppression and how they relate to Black
experiences.

**It will lead us to continue to measure
success based on a white person's
attainment of it, completely disregarding
the identities of marginalized populations.**

*"The white voices yelling that your Blackness
isn't welcomed here even in 2022."*

I moved to Rhode Island in 2012, which was
when I was first introduced to the subtle ways
racism exists. While it wasn't as overt as living
in Mississippi, the policies and structures were
clearly marked with historical contexts of why
they were in place. For instance, people would

say things like "we've always done it this way," in order to not consider how things were always done can sometimes be rooted in white supremacy.

The northeast is indeed an interesting, yet complex place to live. Rainbow flags blow in the wind during pride month. Black Lives Matter signs are plastered in windows of stores and restaurants, but I'm still not able to ignore why people need an explanation to remove the word "Plantation" from the state's name.

"It's a part of our history," they said.

It's as if they don't see us or choose not to. They don't see our Blackness and how Black people have been oppressed and discriminated against because of that very history. A racist white history.

That is the subtleness of living in a racist society.

The white voices yelling that your Blackness isn't welcomed here don't have to be loud. Racism is hidden within the standards, ideals, and norms we've set as a society to prioritize the comfort of white people over my safety, over my Blackness. States across the country continue to silently pass laws to "shield white people from discomfort of racist past" with no acknowledgment of the impact of racism and white people's ability to still benefit from it today (Sue, 2006).

Freire (2019) contends that "to surmount the situation of oppression, people must first critically recognize its causes, so that through transforming action they can create a new situation, one which makes possible the pursuit of a fuller humanity" (p. 47). Yet, ongoing debates continue to take place across the country about whether or not educators should teach Critical Race Theory (CRT) in schools. CRT provides a framework for applying a racial lens to varying systems of oppression (Ladson-Billings, 2019). CRT emphasizes dissecting the differing experiences of people of color living within the United States in relation to white people, which is not something that often happens in predominantly white spaces. In essence, living in a dominantly white society is deemed the norm to classify intelligence and achievement as whiteness, while associating lower class and welfare as Blackness.

This asset-based versus deficit-based categorization positions whiteness at the opposite end of the spectrum in relation to the marginalization of Blackness (Ladson-Billings, 2019). It creates a hierarchy that white people consciously and unconsciously benefit from.

White society tends to do that a lot. Sometimes masked in ignorance, white people can consciously and unconsciously view themselves in a way that maintains power and privilege without taking into account the experiences of marginalized groups and for the sake of white fragility. In response, Black people are forced to bend and code switch just to ensure that other people are comfortable with our Blackness (Haugen, 1956).

But where is our shield?

What policies protect us from enduring harm within these spaces? Within society?

None.

No one can adequately prepare Black people for the racism we experience daily. The inexplicable truth is that society doesn't view our tears and feelings of anguish in the same way as white people's. Unfortunately, they don't hold the same weight or garner similar empathy. In fact, our feelings of distress rarely impact the outcomes of trials, policies, or practices, unlike our white counterparts, even with the data to prove it (Fagan & Meares, 2008). As a result, Black people are forced to swallow our discomfort, which can feel like swallowing nails, and with each gulp, we chip away at a part of ourselves.

...up until the point that we don't anymore.

Until we respond.

Fine Print

Sometimes our unawareness of self within societal contexts, may hinder us from acknowledging the fine print. Here are the key takeaways from Chapter 4:

Now that we've developed a common language and identified where we may be on the journey of ongoing reflection, it is your turn to do the internal work. Using the Terms provided for this chapter and the Terms & Conditions Workbook page 27, respond to the reflection prompts in the space provided. When responding to the prompts, keep in mind that there is no correct or incorrect answer.

CONCLUSION

LIABILITY

Reader,

Welcome back! It's crazy to say this, but after navigating 95 pages of this book and the accompanying workbook, the work of creating an anti-racist society begins here.

At this moment.

Why? You might ask.

I have another story for you.

I pulled up to the Bank of America in Rhode Island at around 1:30 pm. I had thirty minutes to spare until the scheduled closing on my new home, but I wanted to arrive early because, as a business owner, I am aware that the lines are always long. Nervously waiting with all my documents sorted and labeled in folders, I zoned in and out of consciousness—like my time in the Department of Human Services—as the line inched forward. Just as I was starting to calculate how much longer my legs would keep me standing, a voice from behind the plexiglass called out:

"I can help the next person in line."

It was a white woman. She couldn't have been over fifty years old and wore a bright pink blouse; she was still in the holiday spirit on Easter Monday. And because it was almost closing time, I could tell she was over being at work that day. I fumbled with my bank account cards. Five, to be exact. As I inserted one of them into the card reader and inputted the pin, I assured the bank teller, *"I have five accounts with ya'll, business and personal... but my personal savings account doesn't have a card. Is it okay if I insert one of my other cards?"* She had a puzzled look, but slowly nodded her head, yes.

It was closing day for me, and I was excited. I had been anxiously waiting for this day to arrive for months. Finally, I was standing tall and proud in my Black Lemonade sweatshirt with Beyoncé on the sleeve in that bank. I purposely wore my royal blue Balenciaga shoes and hung my Gucci shades on my neckline as confirmation that *I had made it.*

The bank teller proceeded to ask for my ID, which is standard when withdrawing funds. I also preemptively provided her with my account number. I wanted her to believe that I had everything put together. That I was *put together.* I didn't want to give her a reason to question me for what I was about to ask her.

She was silent for a while, which made me uncomfortable.

"Is there a problem with my account?" I asked. Her silence continued for about 3 minutes or so, and she continued to look back and forth between me and her screen.

"The account you mentioned ending in xxxx, it isn't connected with this card. Do you have another?" she asked.

I reminded her that it was a savings account. All of my savings, actually, and it didn't come with a card. She proceeded to look up the account using the information from the license I had handed to her earlier.

"Can you verify the address we have on file?" she asked. As if it wasn't written on my license.

Her questions were fascinating, especially since I'd been to this bank and withdrawn funds more than 100 times. Nevertheless, I provided her with my address.

"Do you have access to the phone associated with the account?" she asked. *"I want to send a code to the phone number that we have on file as a second verification."*

"Sure," I responded as I rolled my eyes.

I provided the bank teller with the code sent to my phone, her fourth attempt to verify my identity. Questions similar to these continued as I stood there verifying my account for what felt like at least 10 minutes. The people in line behind me had all been helped and continued to leave.

I look like the picture on my identification card. My name matches the name on my account verbatim. Still, there was something about her verifying my identity not once... not twice... but at least four times that made me question if she believed that I was capable of withdrawing $47,982.80 from MY savings account.

It was mine and I worked for it.

The bank was just holding the money for me.

That is the subtleness of living in a racist society.

Even after starting my own million-dollar company, putting Dr. Kiara Butler on my bank account, and buying my first home, my Blackness is still the first thing people see when I enter a room. There are still implicit biases that manifest when I navigate spaces, even with all the credentials society says I'm supposed to have. Those credentials don't protect me from the microaggressions and other discriminatory acts I experience daily, and they never will because the system works to protect those who designed it and their likeness.

Maybe that's what the caseworker from the Department of Human Services meant. I didn't fit the profile of a person who needed food stamps, and to this Bank of America teller, I didn't fit the profile of a person with a six-figure bank account either. 10 years later.

Contract Summary

To live in an anti-racist society means to be willing to speak up against policies and laws that harm other people, even if you aren't the one being directly impacted.

As discussed in Chapter 1, there is an interconnectedness between the cycle of abuse and systemic oppression through **power** and control. I felt uneasy the entire time that I was at the bank. Even if some argue that the bank teller's line of questioning was "standard procedure," her condescending tone, untrusting looks, and hesitancy to process my withdrawal still caused harm. At that moment, the bank teller was replicating the social hierarchy as I was inwardly processing my shame, hopelessness, and feelings of being an imposter. In retrospect, she could have explained the reasoning behind her questioning, walked me through the standard process of when a person withdraws large amounts from their bank accounts, or provided assurance in the length of time it took to complete the transaction.

Chapter 2 provided us with best practices for displaying authentic **empathy** through the approach of perspective-taking. Before invalidating my experience at the bank that day, please take a moment to put yourself in my position. Internal reflection is required to truly understand what it means to put ourselves in the place of another person without corrupting the situation with bias. Even if some argue that I should have done something differently, multiple narratives contradicting one another can coexist. In this book, I attempted to describe a narrative where I was positioned as someone capable of maintaining a large bank account. I played into the societal standards and stereotypes that influence our perspective and how we show up in spaces, yet, I don't feel that the bank teller had a deep understanding of my identity and how my identity influences my experiences. That's what I needed at that moment.

We discussed our innate need to belong and our ability to foster genuine **relationships** by providing to others based on their needs and not our own in Chapter 3 because we may create false narratives when interacting with others only on a surface level. Even if some argue that there is no way to build genuine relationships with every single person we meet, there is still the opportunity to create a safe and accepting atmosphere that is inclusive to all. In that moment, the bank teller could have attempted to ask me about my day while I was waiting to complete the withdrawal to process. I would have expressed my excitement about the purchase of my first home. It may have eased the tension and reluctance I was feeling. Societal pressures influence our ability to be vulnerable. It impacts our ability to go beneath the surface and have genuine interactions with people who have identities different than our own.

To live in an anti-racist society means to be willing to unlearn information and processes that continue to replicate systems of oppression.

Chapter 4 provided a life-long process for creating an anti-racist society in two steps:

1. Continuously shifting our **mindset** through gained self-awareness and ongoing reflection.
2. Expanding our cultural knowledge to embrace diverse perspectives and experiences.

Even if some argue that the bank teller's impact was completely unintentional, it is still possible to oppress other people within the varying systems we are trying to overcome. Measuring success based on a white person's attainment of it completely disregards the identities of marginalized populations. It completely ignores my identity, which is the societal messages we continuously receive. After confirming my identity and verifying my bank account, the teller could have taken accountability for her actions or acknowledged her hesitancy, so that I didn't carry the weight of being micro-aggressed. We must do the hard work of identifying and addressing inequities in all spaces we interact within.

To live in an anti-racist society means to take accountability for your contributions to these systems whether intentionally or unintentionally.

We are all responsible.

We all have power.

We all have privilege.

Yet, often, people with institutional power, white people, are unable to reflect on or admit their positionality to power even when reaping the benefits.

After completing this book and the accompanying workbook, can you acknowledge your power and privilege?

Are you able to take accountability for how you've accepted the Terms & Conditions of our society?

Indeed, we can easily overlook the work required to create a more anti-racist society because we generally attempt to address problems and seek solutions outside of ourselves. However, creating an anti-racist society requires the internal work of recognizing what it means to be white or have proximity to whiteness in the United States. The inner work requires that we analyze how white fear derives from the thought of losing power and privilege and the white guilt associated. Suppose society socializes individuals their entire lives to see images of themselves modeled and showcased as the ideal standard. In that case, they may be more inclined to reap society's benefits. *This is not their fault.* They may not realize the power and privilege they hold.

As a queer, same-gender-loving, Black woman who founded an organization grounded in racial equity, I am working hard to compartmentalize my experiences navigating systems of oppression and my rage into action.

In doing so, I am actively creating spaces and resources for people to engage in racial equity conversations while holding the truth that it is not the responsibility of Black people to educate white people on their power or their privilege.

If you were given a chance to change the outcome of a person's life, or if you were given the chance to change policies and structures, would you use your power and privilege to liberate the oppressed?

scan me to commit

Those are the questions I leave you with. This is how I am choosing to end this book because whether you choose to be aware or not, the Terms & Conditions of our society will continue to benefit who they are supposed to.

Definitions Clause

Abomination: an act of disgrace.

American Dream: an equal opportunity provided to achieve success within the United States.

Anti-Blackness: prejudice behaviors, assumptions, or beliefs held against Black people.

Anti-Racist: continuously self-reflecting on individual contributions to injustice on a micro, meso, and macro-level by unlearning and learning how racism operates within the United States and actively addressing and condemning it when witnessed.

Bootstrap Ideology: the belief that hard work is the only determinant of success.

Blaming: the act of wrongly accusing someone.

Cognitive Dissonance: conflicting or inconsistent attitudes, behaviors, and beliefs.

Core Identity: the core identity comprises an individual's intersecting identities, experiences, values, and beliefs. It is the most central aspect of an individual's being and is often referred to as "what makes you, you." Examples: race, gender identity, gender expression, sexual orientation, socio-economic status, ability status, etc.

Denying: the act of refusing to admit the truth.

Economic Abuse: controlling a person's access by utilizing financial resources.

Emotional Abuse: verbal threats and behaviors that manipulate a person's decisions.

Empathy: the acknowledgment, appreciation and deep understanding of various identities and their impact on each individual human experience, to address implicit and explicit biases that affect decision-making and interactions with others.

False Charity: the act of providing resources and opportunities to oppressed populations with the intention of helping them, while still preserving the power of the oppressor.

False Empathy: the ability to understand another person's experiences or circumstances without relinquishing power and control.

Fictive Kinship: a significant relationship built through social ties.

Implicit Bias: the attitudes or stereotypes that unconsciously affect our understanding, actions, and decisions.

Intersectionality: the interconnected nature of social categorizations such as race, class, and gender as they apply to a given individual or group, regarded as creating overlapping and interdependent systems of discrimination or disadvantage.

Institutional Power: the societal approval given to a governing entity to control and make decisions on behalf of other people.

Internalized Oppression: beliefs in negative stereotypes and messaging based on the oppression a person may have experienced firsthand.

Marginalized: social, political, and economic exclusion or insignificance.

Microaggressions: verbal and/or environmental discriminatory behaviors that subtly communicate a prejudice towards a racial group.

Mindset: the expansion of cultural knowledge in order to embrace diverse perspectives and experiences through gained self-awareness and ongoing reflection.

Minimizing: the act of reducing.

Narrative Resiliency: the prioritization of perseverance based on societal standards of strength.

Non-Racist: acknowledging that racism exists within the United States, while still holding individual power by separating self from racism and not condemning it when witnessed.

Opportunity Gap: opportunities afforded to a person based on their race, socio-economic status, or zip-code.

Patriarchy: the prioritization of masculinity within society.

Perspective Taking: the willingness to mitigate bias by seeking to understand another person's experience or circumstances.

Power: the elevation and influence of marginalized populations in order to systematically impact decisions, policies, programs and structures and establish an environment of shared leadership.

Prejudice: a preconceived, unfair, and unreasonable opinion, usually formed without knowledge, that often leads to violent or hateful behaviors.

Privilege: a special advantage, immunity, permission, right, or benefit granted to or enjoyed by an individual, class, or caste.

Racism: any prejudice held or discrimination committed against a racial group that is reinforced by systems of power.

Relationships: the fulfillment of the innate human need to genuinely connect with others and establish a sense of belonging in order to foster a safe and accepting atmosphere that is inclusive to all.

Self-Reliance: an individual's ability to sustain on their own.

Societal Norms: rules that shape a person's values, actions, beliefs, and expectations for self and others.

Sympathy: to feel bad or apologetic for the circumstances or experiences of others.

Systems of Oppression: discriminatory institutions, structures, and norms that are embedded within and reinforced by the structures of our society.

Toxic Masculinity: societal pressures of how manhood should look.

Vulnerability: an openness to being exposed to harm.

White Dominant Narrative: messaging that centers whiteness as the norm, causing others to change their behaviors to fit white standards of appropriateness.

White Fragility: a term used to describe the disbelieving defensiveness, discomfort, anger, or any strong emotions a white person experiences when their ideas about race or racism are challenged.

White Guilt: a term used to describe the shame or remorse felt by a white person when discussing race or racism.

White Supremacy: a culture that associates whiteness as ideal or superior by centralizing a white dominant narrative in systems, structures, and policies.

Intellectual Property Clause

Allen, A. M., Wang, Y., Chae, D. H., Price, M. M., Powell, W., Steed, T. C., Rose Black, A., Dhabhar, F. S., Marquez, Magaña, L., Woods, Giscombe, C. L. (2019). "Racial discrimination, the Superwoman schema, and allostatic load: Exploring an integrative stress coping model among African American women." *Annals of the New York Academy of Sciences*, 1457(1), 104–127. https://doi.org/10.1111/nyas.14188

Babcock, J. C., Waltz, J., Jacobson, N. S., & Gottman, J. M. (1993). "Power and violence: The relation between communication patterns, power discrepancies, and domestic violence." *Journal of Consulting and Clinical Psychology*, 61(1), 40–50.

Bowen, S., Elliott, S., & Hardison Moody, A. (2021). "The structural roots of food insecurity: How racism is a fundamental cause of food insecurity." *Sociology Compass*, 15(7). https://doi.org/10.1111/soc4.12846

Bell, D. (1993). *Faces At the Bottom of the Well: The Permanence of Racism.* Basic Books.

Burke, T. (2017, November 9). MeToo was started for black and brown women and girls. They're still being ignored. *The Washington Post,* 9.

Butler, K. (2021). *Decentering the white gaze in education: The relationship between cultural competence and culturally responsive practices* [Unpublished doctoral dissertation]. Johnson & Wales University.

Chapman, G. D. (2010). *The Five Love Languages.* Walker Large Print.

Crenshaw, K, (1989) "Demarginalizing the Intersection of Race and Sex: A Black Feminist Critique of Antidiscrimination Doctrine, Feminist Theory and Antiracist Politics," *University of Chicago Legal Forum,* Vol. 1989 (1), Article 8.

Crenshaw, K. (1991). "Mapping the margins: Intersectionality, Identity Politics, and Violence Against Women of Color." *Stanford Law Review,* 43(6), 1241–1299.

Crenshaw, K., Ocen, P., Nanda, J. (2015). *Black girls matter: Pushed Out, Overpoliced,*

and Underprotected. Center for
Intersectionality and Social Policy Studies,
Columbia University.

Coates, T. (2015). *Between the World and Me.*
Random House.

Diversity Talks. (2019). Creating space for
conversations about race and identity.
https://www.diversitytalkspd.com/

Diversity Talks. (2019). Uncovering root causes
for inequities in education.
https://www.diversitytalkspd.com/

Diversity Talks. (2020). Measuring cultural
competence: Diversity Talks impact narrative.
https://www.diversitytalkspd.com/

Fagan, J., & Meares, T. L. (2008).
"Punishment, Deterrence and Social Control:
The Paradox of Punishment in Minority
Communities." *Ohio State Journal of Criminal
Law* 6, 173-229.
https://scholarship.law.columbia.edu/cgi/vie
wcontent.cgi?article=2214&context=faculty_sc
holarship

Freire, P., Ramos, M. B., Macedo, D. P., &
Shor, I. (2018). *Pedagogy of the Oppressed.*
Bloomsbury.

Greenwald, A. G., & Banaji, M. R. (1995). "Implicit Social Cognition: Attitudes, Self-esteem, and Stereotypes." *Psychological Review*, 102(1), 4–27. https://doi.org/10.1037/0033-295x.102.1.4

Harris, T. (2002). *Saints, Sinners, Saviors: Strong Black Women in African American Literature*. Palgrave.

Harrison, D. (2004). "An Investigation of Multi-generational Poverty and Barriers to Economic Independence." ProQuest. Retrieved from https://www.proquest.com/openview/1e227f2 4cc274f7c33898acbff1ddc38/1?pq-origsite=gscholar&;cbl=18750&;diss=y

Haugen, E. (1956). *Bilingualism in the Americas: A Bibliography and Research Guide*. American Dialect Society.

Higginbotham, E. B. (1993). *Righteous Discontent: The Women's Movement in the Black Baptist Church, 1880-1920*. Harvard University Press.

Jr., D. D. (1992). "W. E. B. Du Bois and the Idea of Double Consciousness." American Literature, 64(2), 299.

Ladson-Billings, G. (2019). "Just What Is Critical Race Theory, and What's It Doing in a

Nice Field Like Education?" in *Race Is ... Race Isn't: Critical Race Theory and Qualitative Studies in Education*, 7–30.

Moral development. (1992). *Cognitive Development Today: Piaget and His Critics*, 174–185.

Pierce, C. (1970). Offensive mechanisms in *The Black Seventies*, ed. Floyd Barbour, Boston: Porter Sargent.

Prochuk, A. (2018). We Are Here: Women's Experiences of the Barriers to Reporting Sexual Assault. Retrieved from http://www.westcoastleaf.org/wp-content/uploads/2018/10/West-Coast-Leaf-dismantling-web-final.pdf.

Riggle, E. D. B., Drabble, L. A., Bochicchio, L. A., Wootton, A. R., Veldhuis, C. B., Munroe, C., & Hughes, T. L. (2021). Experiences of the COVID-19 pandemic among African American, Latinx, and White sexual minority women: A descriptive phenomenological study. Psychology of Sexual Orientation and Gender Diversity, 8(2), 145–158.

Sue, D. W. (2006). The Invisible Whiteness of Being: Whiteness, White Supremacy, White Privilege, and Racism. In M. G. Constantine & D. W. Sue (Eds.), *Addressing racism:*

Facilitating cultural competence in mental health and educational settings (pp. 15–30). John Wiley & Sons, Inc.

Wacquant, L. (2017). From slavery to mass incarceration. Race, Law and Society, 277–296.

About the Author

Dr. Kiara Butler is a social entrepreneur, keynote speaker, and Founder of Diversity Talks. She is a strong advocate for youth voice, and in her current work she focuses on bringing the voices of marginalized groups to the forefront. Because of her advocacy, she has been recognized for her work in various capacities, such as Forbes 30 Under 30, TEDxProvidence, PBS, EdSurge, The Boston Globe, and The Providence Journal.